A B C
intelligence

Tome 1

A B C
intelligence

complete
with

color

color cat

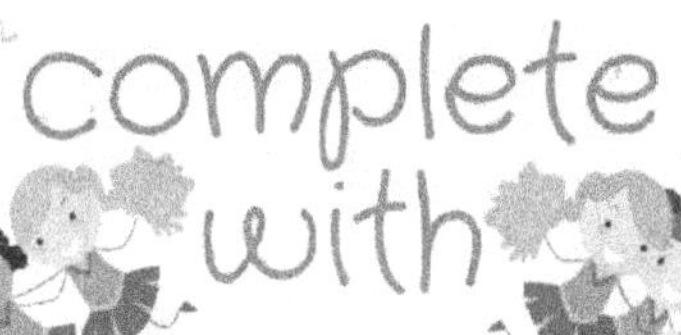

complete with

color horse

complete
with

color dog

color monster

complete with

color

color balloon

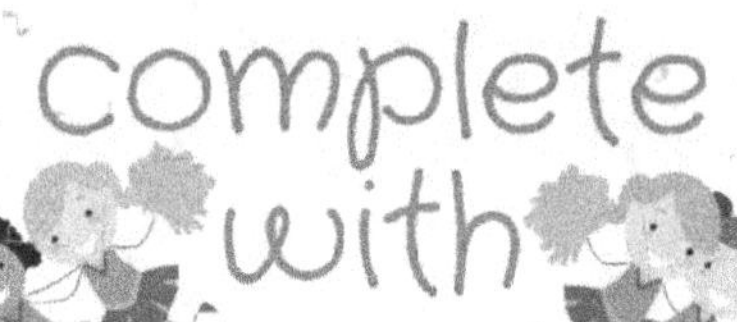

complete with

color balloon

color balloon

complete with

color balloon

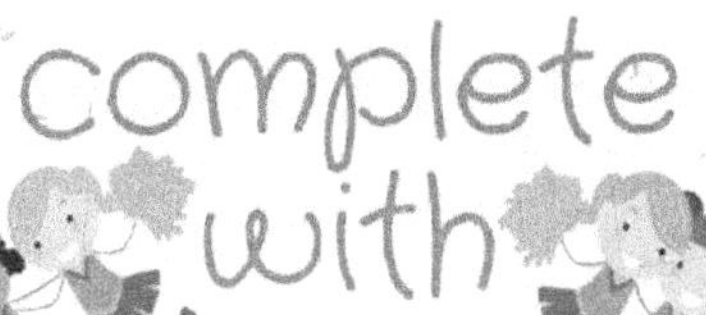

color balloon

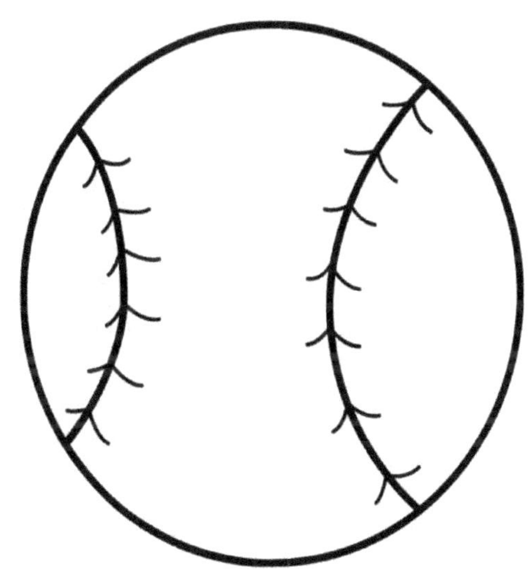

complete
with

color

complete
with

color Pumpkin

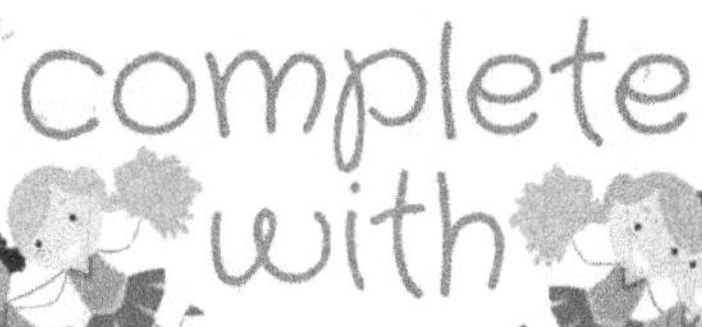

color Pumpkin

complete with

color Pumpkin

complete
with

color Pumpkin

color Pumpkin

color Pumpkin

complete
with

color

complete
with

color

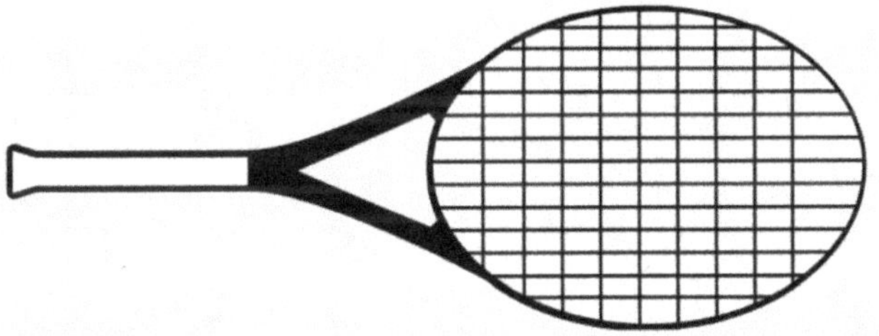

complete
with

..... + ...

=

.....

complete
with

complete
with

complete with

$1 + 1$

$=$

.....

complete with

color

complete with

2 + 2

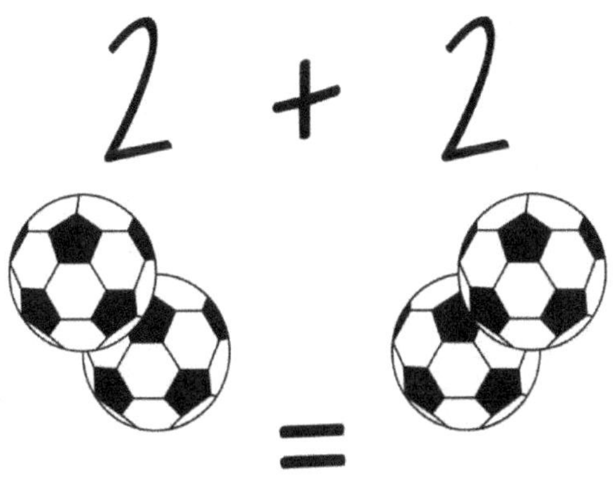

=

.....

3 + 3

complete
with

color

color number 0

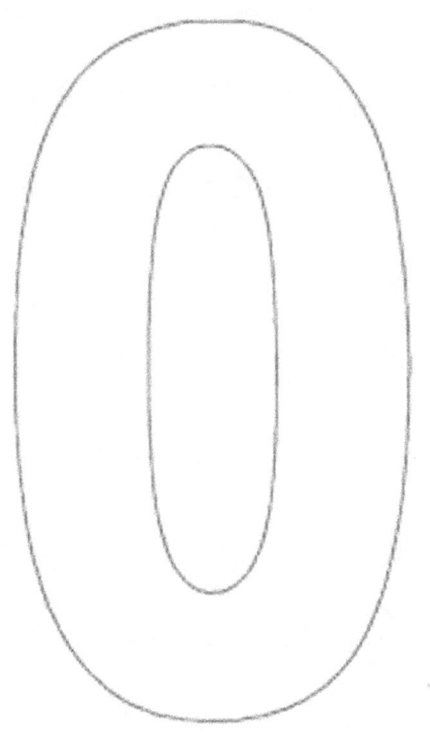

color number 1

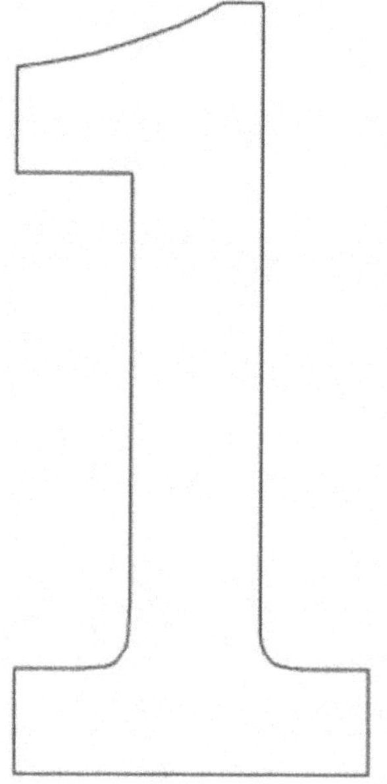

color number 2

color number 3

complete with

color number 4

color number 5

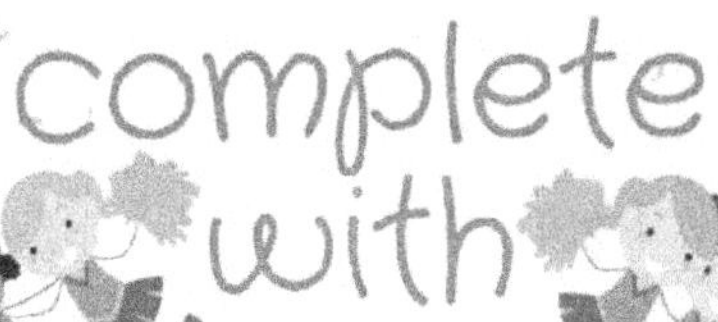

complete with

color number 6

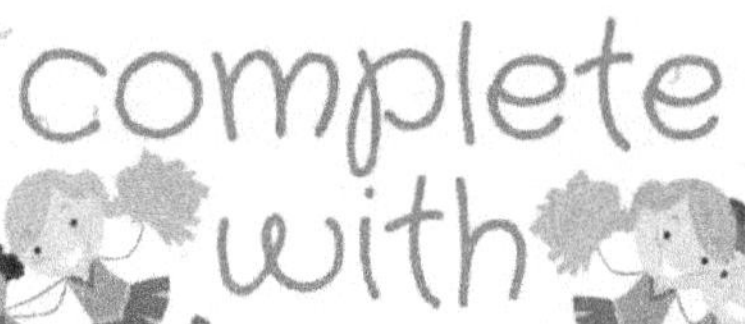

color number 7

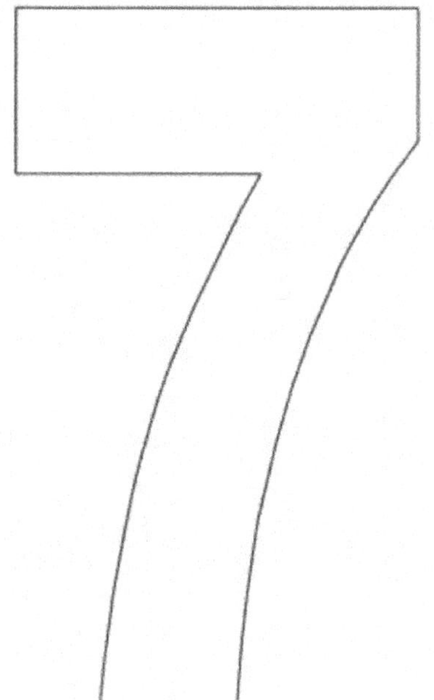

complete with

color number 8

color number 9

color

complete with

color number 3

color number 5

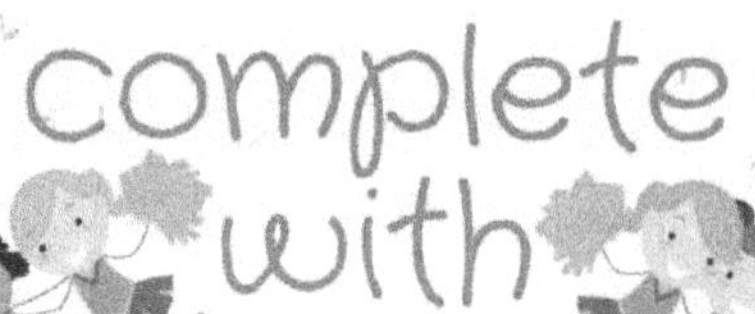

color number 6

complete with

color number 8

color number 3

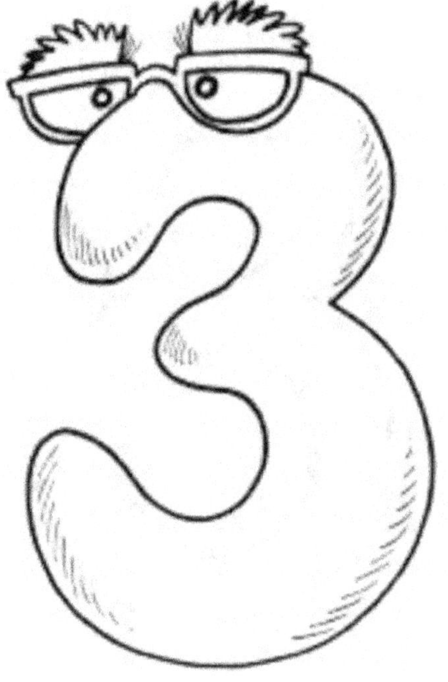

complete
with

color

A B C
intelligence

A B C
intelligence

complete
with

color

complete with

color cat

complete
with

color horse

complete with

color dog

color monster

complete with

color

color balloon

color balloon

color balloon

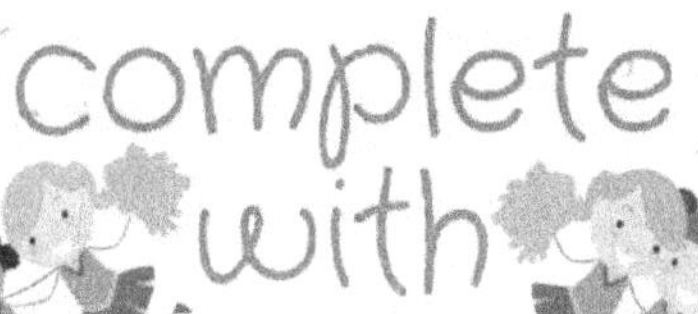

color balloon

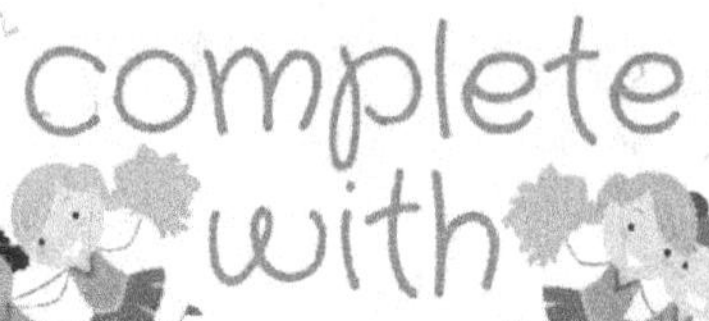

color balloon

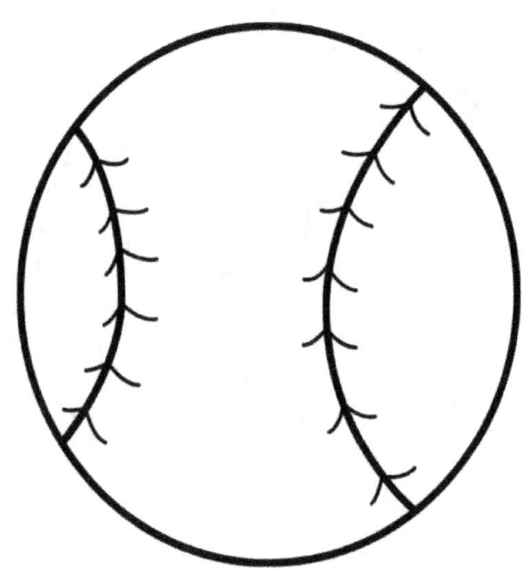

complete with

color

complete with

color Pumpkin

complete with

color Pumpkin

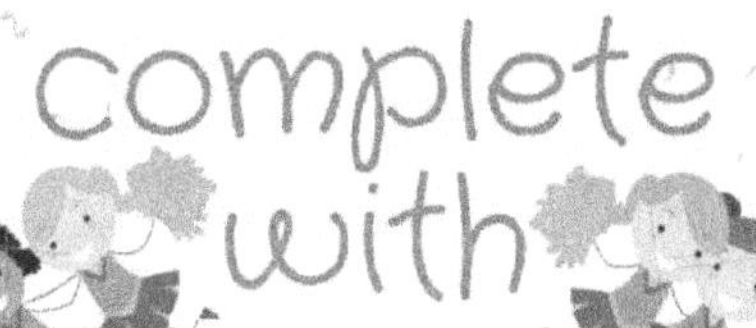

complete with
color Pumpkin

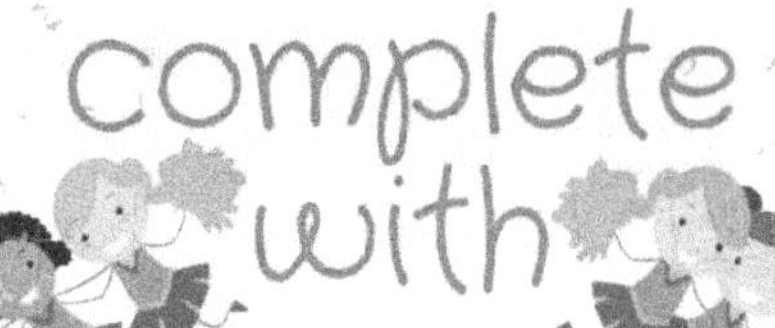

color Pumpkin

complete with

color Pumpkin

complete with

color Pumpkin

complete
with

color

complete
with

color

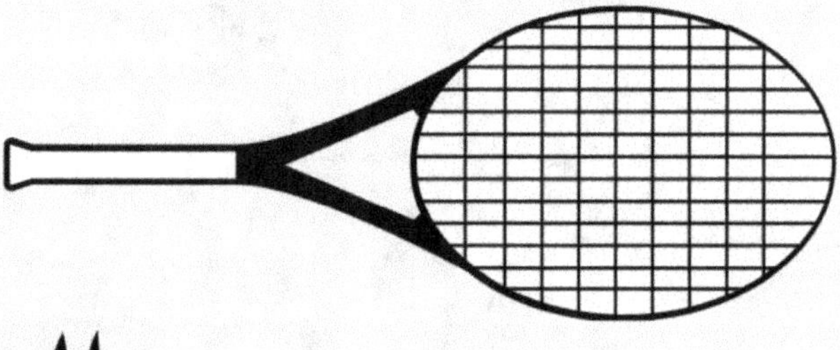

complete
with

..... + ...

=

.....

complete
with

complete
with

complete with

$1 + 1$

=

....

complete with color

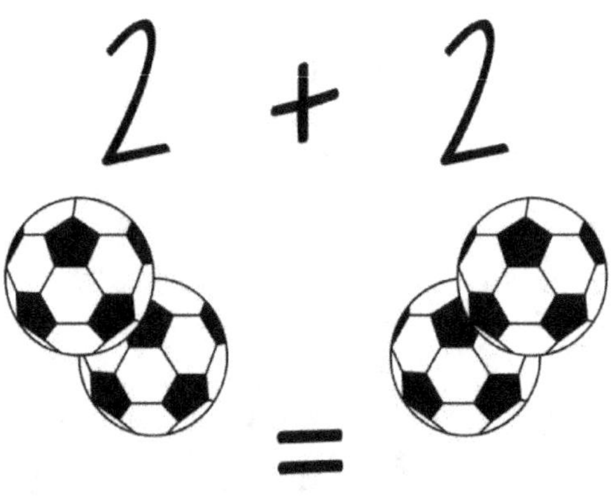

complete
with
2 + 2
=

complete
with
3 + 3
.....

complete with

color

complete with

color number 0

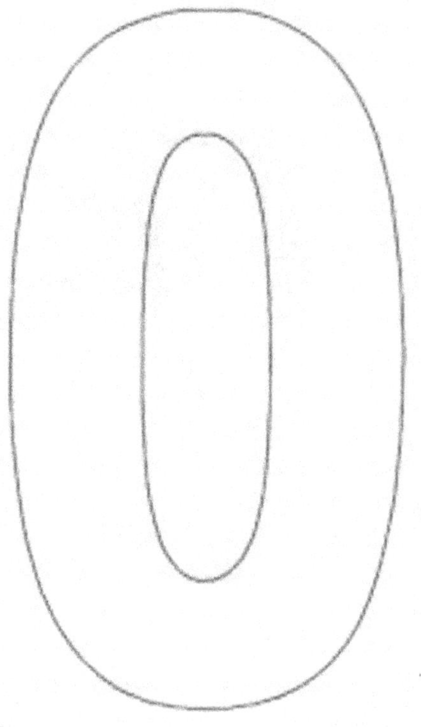

color number 1

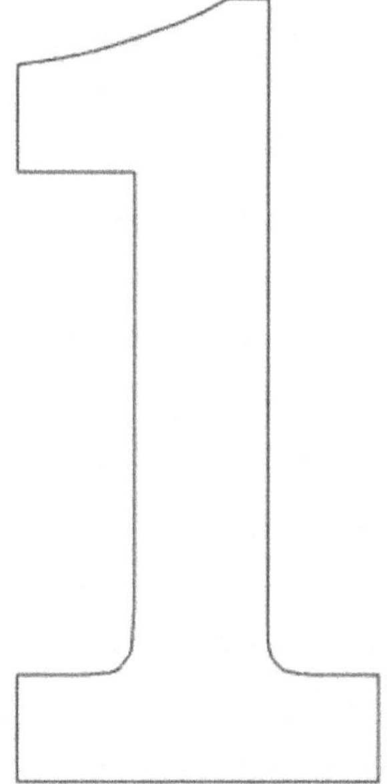

complete with

color number 2

complete with

color number 3

complete with

color number 4

color number 5

color number 6

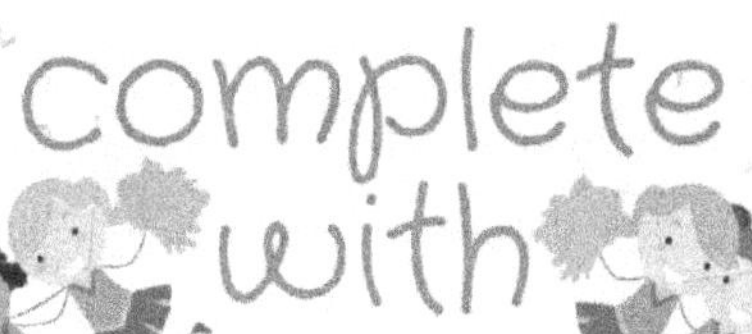

color number 7

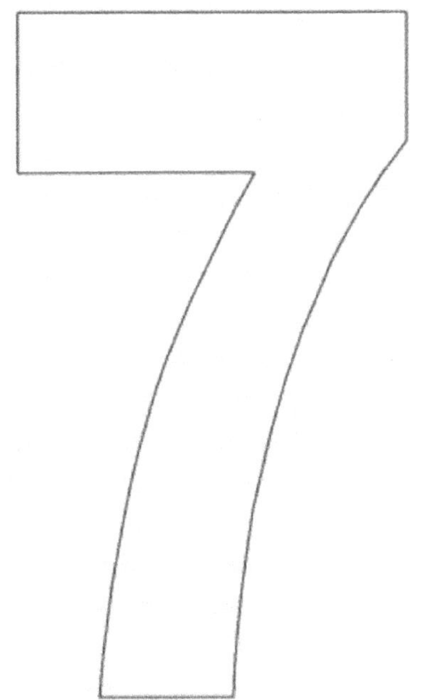

complete with
color number 8

8

complete with

color number 9

complete with

color

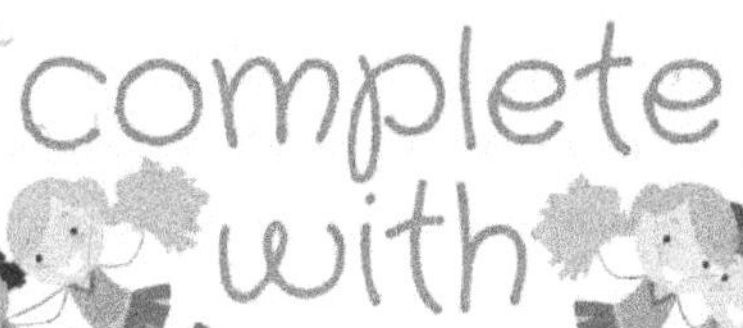

color number 3

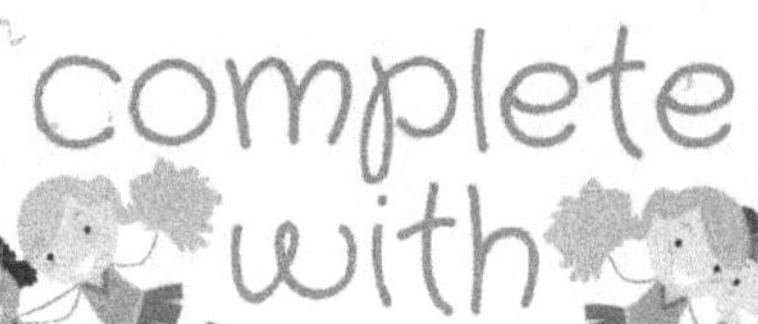

color number 5

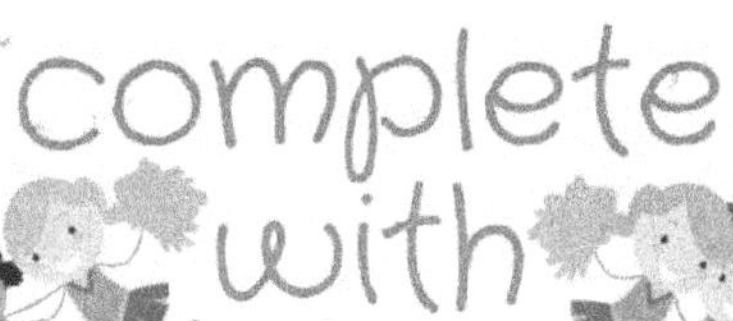

color number 6

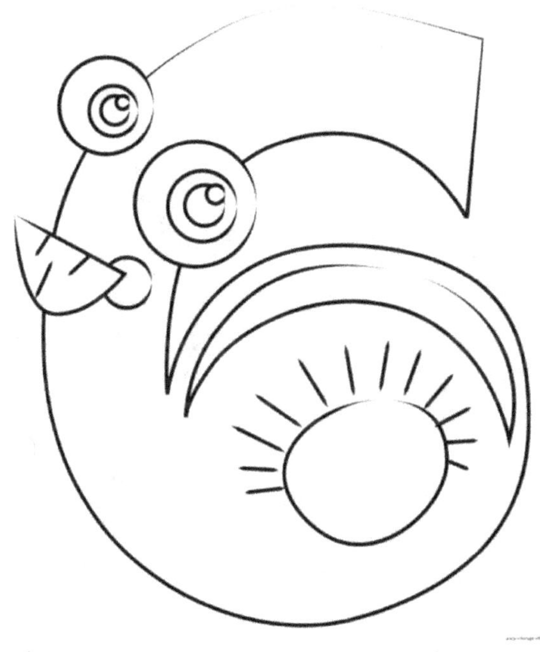

complete with

color number 8

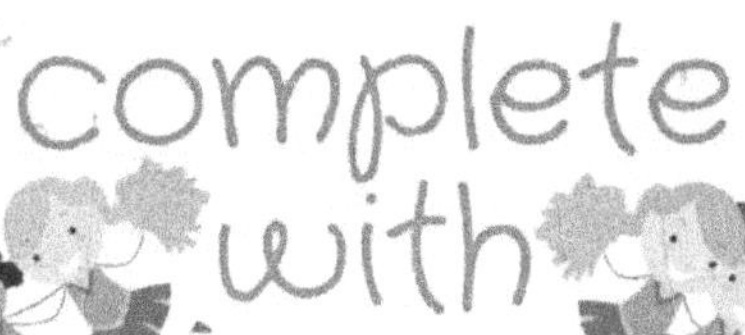

color number 3

complete with color

A B C
intelligence

A B C intelligence

www.ingramcontent.com/pod-product-compliance
Lightning Source LLC
Chambersburg PA
CBHW071230240726
48654CB00009B/985